The World
IN THE TIME OF
Tutankhamen

Dillon Press
Parsippany, New Jersey

Fiona Macdonald

First published in the UK in 1997 by

 Belitha Press Limited, London House, Great Eastern
Wharf, Parkgate Road, London SW11 4NQ

Copyright in this format © Belitha Press 1997
Text by Fiona Macdonald
Map by Robin Carter, Wildlife Art Agency

Published in the United States in 1997 by

Dillon Press
A Division of Simon & Schuster
299 Jefferson Road
Parsippany, New Jersey 07054-0480

Library of Congress Cataloging-in-Publication Data
Macdonald, Fiona.
   The world in the time of Tutankhamen/Fiona Macdonald.
      p.   cm.
   Originally published: London, England: Belitha Press, 1996.
   1. History, Ancient.   2. Civilization, Ancient.   3. Tutankhamen, King
of Egypt.   I. Title.
D80.M25   1997   96-36481
930—dc20

Summary: Tells about the life, death, and tomb of Tutankhamen and what was
happening elsewhere in the world in his time.

ISBN 0-382-39747-9 (LSB)   10 9 8 7 6 5 4 3 2 1
ISBN 0-382-39746-0 (pbk)   10 9 8 7 6 5 4 3 2 1

Editor: Claire Edwards
Art Director: Helen James
Series Design: Roger Miller
Design: Juanita Grout, Rosamund Saunders
and Jamie Asher
Picture Researcher: Diana Morris
Consultant: Sallie Purkis

Printed in Hong Kong

Picture acknowledgments:
Bridgeman Art Library: 1cl; 6-7t, 12 British Museum; 13b Sally Greene;
14r National Museum of India, New Delhi; 15t; 15c National Archaeological
Museum, Athens; 20l Louvre, Paris; 23r Museum of Mankind, London;
24 Giraudon; 25t Sally Greene; 25b Sally Greene; 27b National Archaeological
Museum, Athens; 35c British Museum; 35b National Museum of Australia,
Canberra; 36t Louvre, Paris; 36b Giraudon; 42r Giraudon/Louvre; 43b National
Museum of India, New Delhi; 44b National Archaeological Museum, Athens.
C.M.Dixon: 1c, 5c, 13t, 17b, 19t, 21t, 21c, 25b, 26b, 28l, 31b, 32t, 32c, 33bl,
37, 38t, 41t, 41b, 45b.
Werner Forman Archive: 5tl Egyptian Museum, Cairo; 17t Anthropology
Museum, Veracruz; 22b Provincial Museum, Victoria, B.C.; 33br, 39b British
Museum, London; 43t British Library, London.
Robert Harding Picture Library: front cover, 1cr, 2; 4, 5tr F.L. Kennett; 5b, 6b,
18, 20r; 25c V Southwell; 29t Christopher Rennie; 37t F.L. Kennett; 39t Gary
Hansen; 40 F.L. Kennett; 42l.
Michael Holford: 7b; 14l Musée Cernuschi, Paris; 19b British museum; 27t, 30;
31c British Museum, London; 34.
N.J. Saunders: 45t.
South American Pictures: 16, 23t Tony Morrison.

THE DATES IN THIS BOOK

Today many countries use a calendar that divides time into two separate eras: B.C. (Before Christ) and A.D. (Anno Domino, Latin words that mean "in the year of our Lord"). It was drawn up in 1582 by the head of the Roman Catholic Church. It is based on an earlier calendar invented by the Roman leader Julius Caesar.

You count forward from the year 0 in the A.D. era, and backward from the year 0 in the B.C. era.

B.C. ◄——————— 0 ———————► A.D.
   2000   1000   1000   2000

All dates in this book are B.C.

CONTENTS

ABOUT THIS BOOK

This book tells the story of Tutankhamen and also looks at what was happening all around the world in his time. To help you find your way through the book, each chapter has been divided into seven sections. Each section describes a different part of the world and is headed by a color bar. As you look through a chapter, the color bars tell you which areas you can read about in the text below. There is a time line, to give you an outline of world events in Tutankhamen's time, and also a map, which shows some of the most important places mentioned in this book.

On page 46 there is a list of some of the peoples you will read about in this book. Some of the more unfamiliar words are also listed in the glossary.

THE STORY OF TUTANKHAMEN

Tutankhamen lived in Egypt almost 3,500 years ago. He was born around 1370 B.C. and became pharaoh when he was about nine years old. This book will tell you about life in Tutankhamen's Egypt and what was happening elsewhere in the world in Tutankhamen's time. Because so many important things happened before and after Tutankhamen's short reign, this book also looks at a longer time span, from around 2000 to 1000 B.C.

▼ The mask that covered the face of Tutankhamen's mummy. It is made of pure gold inlaid with semiprecious stones.

AN AMAZING DISCOVERY

Tutankhamen was very young when he became pharaoh, and his reign was short. He did not lead armies into battle or make wise new laws. But today his name and his face are known all over the world. This is because his tomb survived untouched for thousands of years. When archaeologists finally opened it in 1922, they found it full of treasures like the gold portrait mask on the left. These grave goods tell us how rich the Egyptian pharaohs were and show the amazing skills of the craftsmen and women who worked for them.

Tutankhamen is also remembered because his government paid for new temples and statues in many parts of the land and rebuilt the old capital city of Thebes. His workers created some of Egypt's finest monuments, which we can still admire today.

◄ This carved stone panel shows Pharaoh Akhenaton (left), his wife Queen Nefertiti (right), and three of their daughters being blessed by the rays of Aton, the god of the sun.

▼ Two daggers, with their golden scabbards (cases), buried with Tutankhamen in his tomb

◄ Young Tutankhamen probably looked like this carved wood and plaster portrait head, found in his tomb.

A FAMILY OF KINGS

Though not certain, Tutankhamen's father was likely the pharaoh Amenhotep III, one of the richest and most successful rulers in Egypt's history. His mother was Queen Tiy, a strong-minded, intelligent black princess from the rich kingdom of Nubia, south of Egypt. Tutankhamen was the youngest of their three sons and (probably) seven daughters. Because he had two older brothers, he did not expect to rule.

EARLY LIFE

When Tutankhamen was about three, he was sent to live in his oldest brother's palace. His brother's name was Akhenaton. Tutankhamen was brought up with Akhenaton's children.

Like other royal boys, Tutankhamen went to school. He had lessons every morning from palace scribes. They taught him to read the Egyptian picture writing called hieroglyphs. He also learned how to write on papyrus (paper made from reeds), using a pen made from a goose feather and ink made from soot mixed with glue. In the afternoons he practiced swimming and wrestling and was taught to hunt wild animals and fight in war.

◄ Earrings from Tutankhamen's tomb, made of gold and the semiprecious stones carnelian (orange-red), lapis lazuli (deep blue), and turquoise (greenish-blue). He would have worn these on special occasions.

A NEW RELIGION

When their father died, Tutankhamen's brother Akhenaton became pharaoh. Akhenaton was very different from his warlike father. His main interest was religion. He banned the old, magical temple ceremonies and dismissed the priests of Egypt's ancient gods. In their place Akhenaton introduced new rituals for worshiping the god Aton—the life-giving sun. He even moved away from the old royal city of Thebes and built a whole new city, named after Aton, on the opposite bank of the Nile River.

CITY LIFE

Young Tutankhamen probably enjoyed life in Akhenaton's new city, with its palaces and gardens, feasts and festivals. Carvings in his tomb show that he honored Aton, rather than the older, traditional gods, for the rest of his life.

Akhenaton's religious beliefs made the old priests and palace officials very angry. Many Egyptian people threatened to rebel. Tutankhamen's middle brother, Smenkhkare, helped Akhenaton govern the country, but Akhenaton and Smenkhkare both died about 1362 B.C. Now it was the turn of Tutankhamen to rule.

▲ This panel from a painted casket shows Tutankhamen hunting in the desert. He is armed with a bow and arrows and is riding in a chariot pulled by four horses. Chariots like this were a new invention in Tutankhamen's time.

► Tutankhamen's royal throne. At the back you can see a jeweled panel showing Tutankhamen sitting down while his wife puts perfume on his chest.

CROWNED AS A GOD

Tutankhamen was crowned in a splendid ceremony. Priests wore animal-headed masks to represent the gods. They led him through a dark, mysterious temple until he reached the holy throne (see left) where crowns were placed on his head. Once he had been crowned, Tutankhamen became both a god and the chief priest of Egypt.

A YOUNG PHARAOH

Tutankhamen was too young to rule the country. His vizier, Ay, took charge, together with palace scribes and old, wise priests. Now that Akhenaton was dead, they were powerful again. They removed Akhenaton's name from the temples he had built and pulled down his new city. Tutankhamen went back to Thebes, where he lived in a fine new palace. There he began to learn about laws and government and how he should rule. Sadly, we will never know what sort of a pharaoh he would have been, because he died suddenly, aged about 19, in 1352 B.C.

TUTANKHAMEN'S TOMB

Tutankhamen was buried in a tomb hidden deep in the hillside of the Valley of the Kings in Upper Egypt. His body was made into a mummy, then cased in a coffin coated with gold. His burial chamber was filled with everything that a dead pharaoh's spirit might need, from food and drink to books and board games. The tomb walls were covered with magical pictures (such as the hunting scene above) showing Tutankhamen's new life in the world of the dead. Much of our knowledge about ancient Egyptians and pharaohs comes from tomb paintings and goods like these.

◄ Many Egyptian gods were shown with animal heads and human bodies. This painting on papyrus shows a scene in the kingdom of the dead. The jackal-headed Anubis is weighing a dead person's heart against a feather, to see how truthful the person has been. The bird-headed god, Thoth, is writing down the result.

THE WORLD 2000–1000

ABOUT THE MAPS

The maps on this page will help you to find your way around. The big map shows some of the places and peoples mentioned in the text including the following:

- **COUNTRIES** that are different from modern ones, such as CANAAN.
- *Peoples*, such as the *Hittites*.
- **Towns and cities**. To find the position of a town or city, look for the name in the list below and then find the number on the map.

1 San Lorenzo	10 Ur
2 Chavín de Huántar	11 Akhetaten
3 La Venta	12 Karnak
4 Troy	13 Thebes
5 Mycenae	14 Deir el Medineh
6 Knossos	15 Harappa
7 Çatal Hüyük	16 Mohenjo-Daro
8 Jericho	17 Lothal
9 Babylon	18 An-yang

The little map shows the world divided into seven regions. The people who lived in a region were linked by customs, beliefs, traditions, or simply by their environment, although there were many differences within each region. Each region is shown in a different color. The same colors are used in the headings throughout the book to help you match the text with the region.

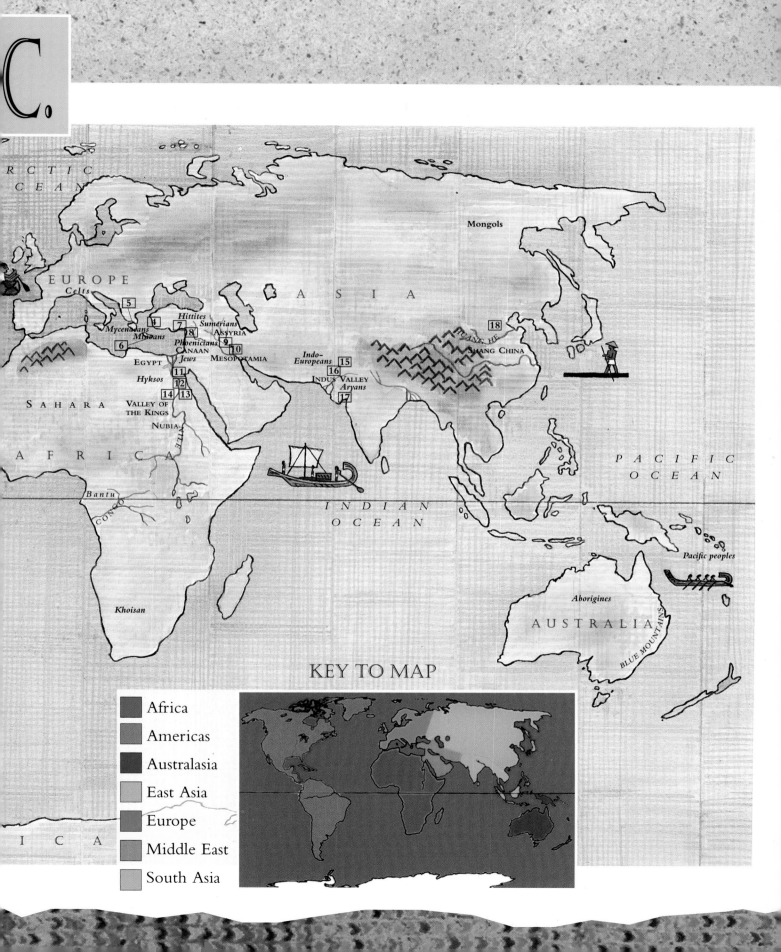

C.

ARCTIC
OCEAN

EUROPE
Celts

Mongols

ASIA

5

Mycenaeans   4   Hittites
Minoans   7   Sumerians
8   ASSYRIA
Phoenicians   9
6   CANAAN   10
Jews   MESOPOTAMIA

EGYPT

Hyksos   11
12

14   13

SAHARA

Indo-
Europeans   15
16
INDUS VALLEY
17   Aryans

18
HUANG HE
SHANG CHINA

VALLEY OF
THE KINGS

NUBIA

AFRICA

Bantu

CONGO

Khoisan

PACIFIC
OCEAN

INDIAN
OCEAN

Pacific peoples

Aborigines

AUSTRALIA

BLUE MOUNTAINS

ICA

KEY TO MAP

Africa
Americas
Australasia
East Asia
Europe
Middle East
South Asia

TIME LINE

| 2000 B.C. | 1800 B.C. | 1600 B.C. |

AFRICA

2000-1000 Khoisan hunter-gatherers are the only inhabitants of southern Africa.

1800 Shaduf used to irrigate fields in Egypt.

1800 Stoneworking industry develops in Ethiopia.

1700 Horse-drawn chariot introduced into Egypt.

1567-1085 New Kingdom era in Egypt.

MIDDLE EAST

2000 Sumerian power collapses but soon begins to revive.

2000 Bronze in widespread use throughout the Middle East.

2000 Babylonians are using calendar based on 60-minute hour and 24-hour day.

1900 Ironworking techniques developed by Hittites in Turkey.

1800 King Shamshi-Adad founds Assyrian empire in Mesopotamia.

1800 First horse-drawn war chariots used in Middle East.

1792-1750 King Hammurabi rules Babylon.

1750-1200 Hittite empire is at height of its power in Turkey and nearby lands.

SOUTH ASIA

2000 In Thailand, villagers hunt wild pigs and gather wild rice, and make fine pottery, bronze axes, and jewelry.

1900 The last mud-brick temples built at Mohenjo-Daro in Indus Valley.

1700 New farming villages, growing wheat and rice, built in foothills of Himalayas.

1600 Mysterious Indus Valley picture writing stops being used.

EAST ASIA

1900 First cities built in China.

2205-1766 Hsia dynasty rules China.

2000 First silk making in China.

1950 First zoo (called the "Park of Intelligence") built in China.

1766-1027 Shang dynasty rules China.

1550 Bronze plow invented in Vietnam

EUROPE

2000-1450 Minoan civilization in Crete is rich and powerful.

1650 Mycenean civilization grows stong in Greece.

2000 First sails used on seagoing boats in the Mediterranean.

2000 Skilled bronzeworkers in many parts of Europe.

2000 First known skis in Scandinavia.

1550 Last stages of rebuilding Stonehenge in England.

AMERICAS

2000 Guinea pigs first domesticated in South America.

1800 First South American villages built in Peru.

1800 Long distance trade networks established in northeastern North America.

AUSTRALASIA

2000 Aboriginal peoples move to settle in eastern Australia.

2000 Settlers from Indonesia reach Melanesia (western Pacific islands).

2000 Aborigines in eastern Australia discover ways of processing poisonous fruit to use as food.

2000-1500 Dingoes (dogs) introduced into Australia from southeastern Asia or possibly India.

500 B.C.   1200 B.C.   1000 B.C.

1498–1483 Queen Hatshepsut rules Egypt.

1158 World's first recorded strike by builders working for pharaohs in Egypt.

1361 Tutankhamen becomes pharaoh.

1500 Village of Deir el Medineh built in Egypt for workers building royal tombs.

1300 Earliest grain-farming villages built in Kenya and Tanzania.

1290–1224 Pharaoh Ramses II builds massive temple at Abu Simbel.

1200 Moses leads Hebrews from slavery in Egypt to new homeland in Israel.

1020 Hebrew kingdom of Israel founded.

1100 Iron replaces bronze as the most important metal for weapons and tools.

1100 Phoenicians invent alphabet of letters on which modern European script is still based.

1500 Aryans invade northern India; they introduce bronze weapons and war chariots into India.

1000 Ironworking introduced to India.

1500 Horses, camels, and donkeys introduced into northern India.

1400–1000 First bronze tools and simple drums made in Malaya, Indonesia, and also in Vietnam.

1500 Indus Valley civilization collapses.

1450 Hindu worship of god Brahma slowly spreads through India.

1500 Chinese use pictograph script (picture writing).

1200 Bells cast from bronze in China.

1500 Rice first grown using paddy-field (flooded field) system in Korea.

1200 Soybean cultivation becomes widespread in China.

1500 First silk-making in China.

1100 Mouth organ invented in China.

1450 Mycenaeans invade Minoan Crete.

1250 Traditional date of Trojan War.

1250 Lion Gate built at Mycenae, Greece.

1000 Ironworking becomes widespread in Greece and central Europe.

1200 End of Mycenaean civilization in Greece.

1400 Sunflowers first cultivated in North America.

1200 Chavín civilization develops in Peru.

1000 New Adena civilization in Ohio Valley in North America.

1500 First Maya people settle in clearings in the rain forests of Guatemala.

1500 Earliest metalwork in South America.

1200 Beginnings of Olmec civilization in Mexico.

1300 Settlers from New Guinea migrate to Fiji.

1000 Long-distance trade routes develop in Australia.

1500 Aboriginal hunters invent new methods for trapping fish and eels.

1100 Settlers from Fiji reach Tonga and Samoa.

Most of the dates shown in this Time Line are approximate.

AROUND THE WORLD

The world was a very restless place in Tutankhamen's time. In some parts, such as Egypt and China, there were civilizations that had existed in one place for thousands of years. Often these had grown up along river valleys, where there was plenty of fertile land. People settled there and built towns that grew into big cities with powerful rulers. But in many other regions—southern Africa, Asia, Europe, and the Pacific—groups of migrating peoples were on the move, in search of a new home.

Sometimes, small tribes fought richer neighbors just for a share of good land. But most migrations were on a very large scale. For example, the Indo-European peoples left their home in southern Russia to settle in India, Greece, central Europe, and Iran. Often migrants attacked and conquered earlier civilizations, setting up new nations and introducing their own language, technology, and beliefs.

◀ This stone pillar was used to mark the borders of a rich man's land. It shows King Nebuchadnezzar I, who ruled Babylon around 1140 B.C., together with gods and monsters.

TOWNS AND EMPIRES

MIDDLE EAST

The first towns in the world were built in the Middle East, at Çatal Hüyük (in Turkey) and Jericho (in Jordan), between around 8000 and 6500 B.C. They were both important centers for religion, crafts, and trade. Çatal Hüyük was abandoned about 5000 B.C., but Jericho was still rich and busy in Tutankhamen's day. By then it had been rebuilt and enlarged many times.

After around 2000 B.C., Babylon, in Mesopotamia (part of present-day Iraq) became the most important town in the Middle East. It was the capital city of a great empire founded by King Hammurabi (see page 20), who ruled from about 1792 to 1750 B.C.

WEALTH AND POWER

AFRICA

Tutankhamen lived during an era called the New Kingdom, which lasted from 1567 to 1085 B.C. It began when Egyptian armies drove invaders, called the Hyksos, out of their land. After that, Egyptian pharaohs, including Tutankhamen's father, set out to rebuild their kingdom's wealth and power. They conquered an empire that stretched from present-day Sudan to the borders of Turkey. They built huge monuments to thank the gods for their success, and as memorials to their own power. You can see a pharaoh attacking his enemies in the stone carving (right).

▲ A cave painting from Algeria. It shows men and women in dry countryside on the borders of the Sahara. It was probably painted between 5000 and 1000 B.C.

NATIONS ON THE MOVE

In some parts of Africa, whole nations were on the move. A change in the climate made the Sahara drier, so the peoples living there moved south in search of better grazing for their flocks of sheep and herds of horses and cattle. Groups of Bantu people from the forests of West Africa also left their homes to look for new land. They traveled south through the Congo Valley and eastward toward the coast.

► In this stone carving, Pharaoh Ramses III is killing an enemy with a war club. Underneath, craft workers carved the names of cities he conquered.

THE SHANG EMPIRE

EAST ASIA

In northern China a powerful empire grew up in the fertile Huang He (Yellow River) valley, ruled by emperors from the Shang dynasty. Skilled artisans, priests, and scribes lived in the empire's rich cities. Below, there is an example of fine Shang craft work.

In the countryside, peasants grew wheat and millet. Rice was grown in the empire's warmest, rainiest lands. Fierce warriors rode about in horse-drawn chariots, keeping control of conquered peoples. They also helped the emperors defend the empire from invaders, such as the Mongol tribes from the north.

◀ This bronze jug from Shang China is shaped like a tiger. It was used to hold wine, which was poured out as an offering to dead ancestors. This was an important part of religious worship.

THE INDUS VALLEY

SOUTH ASIA

From around 2500 B.C., the Indus Valley (in present-day northern India and Pakistan) was home to a great civilization. The people who lived there were traders and lived in towns. More than a hundred sites have been discovered so far, scattered over a vast area of about 400,000 square miless. The biggest cities, such as Mohenjo-Daro, Harappa, and Lothal, had streets that were carefully laid out on a grid plan, and complicated drainage systems. There were also huge grain stores, temples, and ceremonial baths. Town dwellers had money to spend on art and entertainment, as the little statue of a richly-jeweled dancing girl (see right) shows.

The Indus Valley civilization collapsed around 1500 B.C. No one knows why. It may have been destroyed by invading tribes. Or it may have been destroyed by a change in the climate, by earthquakes, or by floods.

▶ A copper statue of a dancing girl. It is about 6 inches high and was made by craft workers from the city of Harappa in the Indus Valley, around 2000 B.C.

▲ The Lion Gate at the entrance to the king's palace at Mycenae in southern Greece. The gateway and the lions above it are made from huge blocks of stone.

MINOAN STYLE

EUROPE

In southern Europe, from around 2000 B.C., Minoan people lived in great comfort and style on the island of Crete. You can see a glamorous Minoan noblewoman in the picture on the right. The Minoans ruled an empire that included many Mediterranean islands, as well as city-states on the shores of southern and central Greece. They traded with the Egyptians and Middle Eastern peoples, and sometimes fought against them, too. Minoan power was weakened after a volcano called Thera erupted on an island near Crete around 1450 B.C. Dust from the volcano blotted out the sun, damaged the land, and caused a shortage of food.

GREEK WARRIOR KINGS

On the Greek mainland, proud warrior kings ruled rival city-states. A city-state was a city or town, together with the surrounding farms and fields. Greek kings defended their land by building strong forts with massive gateways, like the one you can see on the left. They led their armies to attack Minoan Crete in 1450 B.C., and waged a famous war against the city of Troy (in present-day Turkey) around 1250 B.C.

◄ Noblewomen in Minoan Crete wore elegant clothes. This fresco (wall painting) is from a royal palace. It shows a young woman wearing a fitted top and a long, full skirt. Her dark curly hair is loose, and she has large hoop-shaped earrings.

FARMERS AND HUNTERS

In northern Europe there were no cities. Instead, farmers and hunters lived in villages and on farms. Because they left no written records, we do not know much about their society. But grave goods show us that there were a few very rich people, probably warrior chiefs. There were many rich merchants, too, who traded in amber and gold.

Around 1200 B.C. early Celtic settlers arrived from eastern Europe, bringing with them a new civilization. The Celts built forts on the tops of hills and traded with southern Europe for wine.

RIVER VALLEYS: SETTLED VILLAGES

AMERICAS

In Tutankhamen's time there were many different civilizations in North and South America. These included the Inuit seal hunters of the icy Arctic north and the peoples of the steamy Amazon rain forest, who survived by gathering insects and wild plants. Many of these hunters lived nomadic lives, always moving on to new land in search of food. But by Tutankhamen's time some Native American peoples had settled in sheltered, well-watered river valleys, where they built villages, cleared fields, and planted crops.

In the wide valleys of the Mississippi and Ohio rivers, people lived by growing sunflowers, gourds, and pumpkins, and by long-distance trade. Perhaps as early as 1100 B.C. they began to build massive earthworks, which they used as religious meeting places and for defense.

A SPLENDID MEXICAN CITY

In Mexico the Olmec civilization became powerful around 1200 B.C. Its capital city and religious center was at San Lorenzo. The Olmecs controlled rich farmlands. Unlike many other parts of Mexico, crops grew very well there, and harvests were good, thanks to flood water from rivers and seasonal rains. Because of this the Olmec people rarely were short of food. Their population increased, and the Olmec nation grew strong and wealthy.

The Olmec rulers of San Lorenzo paid for many enormous monuments to be built, such as earth-mound temples, ceremonial lakes, and stone thrones. Artisans also carved eight colossal heads, each one of a different king. Archaeologists have found the remains of over 200 houses in the center of San Lorenzo. This suggests that well over 1,000 people lived there, making San Lorenzo one of the biggest cities of the time.

▲ These well-armed warriors were carved onto stone at a ceremonial center in Peru known as Chavín de Huántar.

MOUNTAIN HOMES

From around 2000 B.C., people began to build the first villages in South America, in the Andes region. By around 1200 B.C. these villages had stone temples, open air meeting spaces, and channels bringing water from mountain streams. Most had markets where mountain produce, such as potatoes, could be exchanged for fish and shells from the coast. Warriors guarded the villages and helped rulers to take control of more land.

▲ A massive head carved from stone by Olmec craft workers at San Lorenzo. It is more than 7 feet high and weighs about 20 tons. It shows an Olmec king wearing a helmet.

UNINHABITED ISLANDS

For centuries no one lived on the islands of the Pacific Ocean. But around 2000 B.C., groups of people left their homelands in southeastern Asia, Indonesia, and Papua New Guinea and set off toward the unknown, in search of more food and new land. They made long, dangerous ocean journeys, sometimes over 1,500 miles, in fragile wooden canoes. To help them navigate, they watched wind and wave patterns, the flight of seabirds, and the movement of clouds and the stars. Soon after Tutankhamen's time they had reached Fiji, Tonga, and Samoa and had set up thriving communities there. The Pacific settlers brought many ideas and customs from their old homelands, including belief in spirits like the ones pictured below.

▼ Ancient spirit faces painted on the wall of a modern house in Papua New Guinea. Beliefs in spirits like these have survived since Tutankhamen's time.

EXPLORING NEW LAND

AUSTRALASIA

The Aborigines first settled in Australia around 40,000 B.C. At first they lived along the coast, but as the sea level rose and flooded their homes, they moved inland. They traveled from camp to camp as they hunted and explored. By Tutankhamen's time they had made a network of long-distance routes between camp sites, holy places, and hunting grounds. Aborigine sailors also traded with India and southern Asian lands.

FAMOUS RULERS AND LEADERS

Today, in democratic countries, if people do not like the way their rulers behave, they can vote to remove them from power. But in Tutankhamen's time, whether rulers were good or bad, they usually stayed in power for life. Most rulers claimed that the gods had given them the right to rule the country. Some believed that they were descended from the gods or were gods themselves.

In lands such as Egypt and the Middle East, scribes proudly recorded the deeds of their rulers. In other parts of the world, myths and legends tell us the names of early kings. But in many regions no written records were kept. We do not know the names of the rulers who lived there. But by looking carefully at archaeological remains and ancient traditions, we can discover some of the things they did.

◄ This huge statue of Ramses II is carved out of solid rock. It stands outside his most famous temple at Abu Simbel in southern Egypt. The temple was specially built so that twice a year the sun's rays shone through the doorway, showing statues of the gods carved on the inner walls.

RULERS OF THE GODS

The Egyptians were taught
that their pharaohs were gods in human form.
Pharaohs were worshiped, respected, and feared.
As chief priests, war leaders, and guardians of law
and order, they had many duties. They planned
conquests, made peace treaties, and gave orders
to thousands of government officials. Many of
Egypt's greatest rulers lived in the New Kingdom
period. One example is Queen Hatshepsut, who
ruled (1498–1483 B.C.) on behalf of her stepson,
Pharaoh Thutmose III. Even when he was grown
up, she refused to hand over power. Under her
rule, Egypt began to trade with and explore
distant lands.

◄ Queen
Hatshepsut had
a huge temple
built as a
memorial to
herself on the
the banks of
the Nile River.
This statue of
the queen is
from the
temple.

RAMSES THE GREAT

Ramses II ruled from 1290 to 1224 B.C. and
was one of Egypt's greatest pharaohs. He ruled
for nearly 67 years, had about 90 children, and
left more monuments than any other Egyptian
king. He fought long wars against the Hittites,
and scenes from his battles were cut in stone
in many of his temples. Ramses finally made
peace with the Hittites about 1286 B.C., and
married a Hittite princess. To strengthen
friendship between nations,
many pharaohs married
hundreds of official wives.

► A panel made to decorate a
musical instrument called a lyre.
The King of Sumer, at the top,
receives enemy prisoners. Sumer is
shown at the height of its power.
By Tutankhamen's time, Sumerian
power had collapsed, and Egypt
and Babylon were the strongest
powers in the Middle East.

WAR LEADERS

Rival tribes constantly
fought over the lands of the Middle East,
which meant that the earliest rulers were war
leaders. Victory in war brought vast riches, and
some of these treasures were buried with kings
when they died. Some of the most splendid royal
tombs were built at Ur, capital of the Sumerian
Empire. The empire was destroyed by invaders
some time around 2000 B.C.

WARRIOR AND LAWMAKER

King Hammurabi (ruled 1792–1750 B.C.) was a successful warrior. He conquered a vast empire, which he ruled from the city of Babylon. But he became even more famous as a lawmaker. He collected all the laws from different parts of his empire and arranged them in one single code. This code covered everything from robbery and murder to fair trade, paying doctors, getting married, hiring workers, and buying slaves. Hammurabi had his laws carved on a tall stone pillar, which you can see below.

► Here you can see a stone portrait of a ruler priest, from the city of Mohenjo-Daro. He is wearing a jeweled headband and armband and an embroidered robe.

◄ This stele (stone pillar) shows the Babylonian sun god, Shamash, dictating laws to King Hammurabi. The lower part of the pillar is carved with Hammurabi's laws. They ordered harsh punishments for anyone who disobeyed them.

RULER PRIESTS
The Indus Valley

civilization was rich and well organized, with strongly built, carefully planned cities. This suggests that there were good leaders, but we do not know their names. The largest Indus Valley cities had homes for about 40,000 people, with wide streets leading to huge religious buildings at the city centers. But no remains of palaces have been found. Historians think this means that the Indus Valley rulers were priests, rather than kings.

THE ARYANS

Around 1500 B.C. the Aryans invaded northern India. We know about their society from a series of poems called the Vedas, some of the oldest surviving poems in the world. The Vedas describe a society led by kings and warrior heroes, organized into four separate groups called castes. Each caste had a different task to perform, as priests, warriors, merchants, or farmers.

◄ This is the throne room in the royal palace at Knossos on the island of Crete. The palace was built for Minoan kings, but we do not know if King Minos existed in real life. He may be only a name in ancient stories and legends.

▼ A gold mask covering the face of a dead king, found in a tomb at Mycenae in Greece. At first, archaeologists thought it might belong to legendary King Agamemnon, but in fact it was made for a king who died earlier.

HERO KINGS

EUROPE

We do not know the names of any northern European rulers who lived in Tutankhamen's time, but archaeologists have found their remains in huge stone tombs. We know more about rulers in southern Europe from Greek legends. The remains of palaces and tombs also survive in many parts of Greece.

According to Greek legend, King Minos was the ruler of Crete. His name is used to describe the civilization that flourished there from around 2000–1450 B.C.. Four huge Minoan palaces have been found. The largest, at Knossos, had over 1,300 rooms, including the king's throne room, storerooms, bathrooms, and lavatories. Many rooms were beautifully decorated with brightly painted walls.

POWERFUL PRIESTESSES

Women often played an important part in decision making in Mediterranean lands. As priestesses they advised rulers and even claimed to be able to see into the future. In Troy, the legendary priestess Cassandra gave accurate warnings that her city would be destroyed in war.

THE TROJAN WAR

Ancient Greek poems describe a war fought around 1250 B.C. between the Greeks and the Trojans, who lived in present-day Turkey. The poems say that King Agamemnon of Mycenae was leader of the Greeks. At Mycenae there are the remains of a royal fortress, built on a hilltop and protected by huge gates (see page 15). King Agamemnon could have lived there. Similar fortress cities have been found elsewhere in Greece.

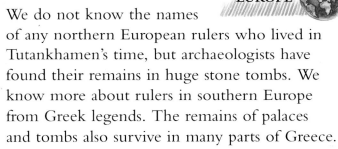

A LEGENDARY KING

EAST ASIA

According to ancient legends, the first Chinese ruler was Yu the Great, king of the Hsia dynasty. But, because there are no written records, we cannot prove that he ever lived. We know more about the next ruling family because Chinese scholars invented picture writing during their reign. These kings belonged to the Shang dynasty and came to power around 1766 B.C. The Shang kings ruled with the help of vast armies and fierce warlords. They encouraged crafts, farming, building, and new technology, but many Chinese people thought them cruel.

▲ This portrait of Yu the Great was painted by a Chinese artist who lived thousands of years after Yu's reign and imagined how Yu looked.

► This mask has a human face and an eagle beak. The Native American Bella Coola people believed that four carpenters were told by their Creator to carve the very first humans. They flew to earth disguised as birds and animals. This is one of the carpenters.

BURIALS AND SACRIFICES

In one of the Shang dynasty's capital cities, called An-yang, archaeologists have found the remains of a magnificent royal palace. It stands on top of a huge burial pit containing 852 people, 35 dogs, 18 sheep, 15 horses, 10 oxen, and 5 war chariots. They were all sacrificed before the palace was built to bring good fortune to the Shang kings.

SKILLFUL CHIEFS

AMERICAS

Rulers in North and South America had different duties, depending on how their people lived. Some were brave fighters, some were clever hunters, and others were healers and priests, called shamans. Many Native American peoples were led by teams of chiefs. They were usually experienced warriors and wise men. Each member of the ruling team offered his own experience and skills to help the community survive. Some Native American leaders claimed to have magical powers that let them communicate with the spirit world.

▲ A royal throne from the Olmec city of La Venta, Mexico. It is carved with the figure of a king wearing a large crown and a necklace.

KINGS AND CAPTIVES

Leaders of other American peoples, such as the Olmecs of Mexico, were army commanders and priests. They organized soldiers to defend their peoples' homes and farms and to conquer new territory. They were also in charge of planting crops and distributing food. They made laws to help villagers live peacefully with one another. Often the palaces where they lived were places of worship as well as splendid homes. It was the duty of the leaders to kill captives taken in battle and to offer them to the gods.

From the evidence of massive statues, Olmec kings may have taken part in sacred ballgames. In these games the movement of the ball was supposed to copy the movement of the sun as it traveled across the sky. Winners became heroes, but losers were killed as sacrifices.

RULERS FROM THE SEA

AUSTRALASIA

We do not know the names of any people who lived in Australia or the Pacific Islands in Tutankhamen's time. But in Australia, myths tell of a god-leader called the Djanggawul Brother. He arrived from the sea with his two sisters and taught the Aborigines to dig waterholes and find food. He also taught them new religious ceremonies. Real leaders probably behaved in this way, too.

Among the Pacific Islanders the most powerful people may have been the leaders of groups of settlers who led their families and friends across the ocean in search of new land.

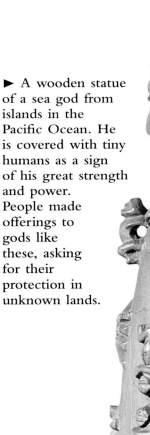

► A wooden statue of a sea god from islands in the Pacific Ocean. He is covered with tiny humans as a sign of his great strength and power. People made offerings to gods like these, asking for their protection in unknown lands.

HOW PEOPLE LIVED

▼ In this Egyptian wall painting, you can see a farmer and his wife hard at work. He is steering a plow pulled by two oxen. She is scattering seeds of wheat. At the bottom of the picture, there are date-palm trees, planted beside an irrigation ditch.

All around the world, civilizations had to produce enough food to feed their growing populations. Reliable supplies of food and water were especially important for craft workers, merchants, government officials, and other town dwellers. These people no longer grew their own food, but had to buy it instead.

Although towns were increasingly important, most people still lived in the countryside. Some were hunters and gatherers. Many more were farmers. All the world's major food crops, including wheat, corn, rice, and yams, had been cultivated by around 1500 B.C. Most farm animals, including cows, pigs, sheep, goats, horses, and dogs, had been domesticated. But rulers and farmers were always looking for better ways to farm and extra crops to grow.

A RICH LAND

AFRICA

Tutankhamen lived in one of the richest countries on earth. Most of Egypt's land was desert, but every year the Nile River flooded its banks, spreading a layer of sticky black mud on either side. This fertile soil produced good crops of wheat, barley, fruit, and vegetables. People called Egypt "the gift of the Nile." The Egyptians also sent soldiers and miners to work in gold and copper mines in nearby lands.

Pharaohs and top government officials lived in grand palaces, with dining halls, shower rooms, flower-filled gardens, and ponds. Ordinary people lived in one-roomed houses of sun-dried mud brick, with stairs leading to a flat roof where they could sleep on hot nights.

Because Egypt was hot all year round, people wore few clothes. Children usually wore nothing at all, men wore loincloths or short skirts, and women wore loose robes. Clothes were made of fine linen or of hemp. Men and women shaved their heads, possibly to get rid of lice. They wore thick wigs, which they perfumed on festival days.

HUNTERS AND GATHERERS

In Tutankhamen's time the first farming villages were built in present-day western Africa, Kenya, and Tanzania. Houses of earth had roofs made of grass and leaves. In other parts of Africa, most people lived by gathering wild foods, by hunting in rain forests, or by fishing. The far south of Africa was almost uninhabited, apart from a few bands of Khoisan hunters and gatherers.

▲ This cave painting of a cow is from North Africa and was made between about 6000 and 1000 B.C. Herdsmen grazed cattle on the edges of the Sahara. They also gathered wild fruit and grains to eat.

◄ Rich Egyptian homes were full of lovely objects. Here artisans make gold and silver vases. First they hammer a vase into shape, then they decorate it with engraved patterns, and finally they give it a polish.

BREAD, OIL, AND WINE

MIDDLE EAST

In the marshy soils of Mesopotamia, farmers grew wheat, vegetables, and fruit. They kept oxen to pull plows and caught fish and water birds in irrigation ditches and canals. They built houses of reeds and sun-dried mud brick, dug from the riverbanks.

On higher ground, in Canaan and Assyria, farmers grew barley for bread, sesame for oil, and grapevines to make wine. On mountain slopes they tended forests of cedar trees. The sweet-smelling wood from these trees was used to decorate rich homes, palaces, and temples in many Middle Eastern lands.

BUSTLING TOWNS

Busy, prosperous trading towns where scribes, merchants, doctors, lawyers, and craft workers lived and worked could be found in many parts of the Middle East. Kings also built huge palaces, fine gardens, and splendid temples.

Rich townspeople lived a leisurely life. In Mesopotamia, royal tombs have been found containing all sorts of objects, from board games to musical instruments. Women wore gold rings on their fingers and in their hair, and beads made of a red stone called carnelian. They also used makeup, which was kept in little shells.

BATHROOMS AND BRONZE

SOUTH ASIA

Indus Valley homes were built of mud bricks. They were large and well-planned, with five or six rooms arranged around a central courtyard. Townspeople had piped water, and bathrooms and lavatories connected to a central drainage system—the most advanced in the world. Lothal, a city on the coast, was the main port. It had a brick-built harbor and big warehouses. Indus Valley merchants exchanged local products, such as timber, elephant ivory, spices, and cotton cloth, for semiprecious stones and tin, which they needed to make bronze.

◄ A large meetinghouse built from reeds. This photo was taken in present-day Iraq, but reed houses were already being built in this style in Tutankhamen's time.

RICH LAND

Crops grew well in the Indus Valley. Farmers harvested wheat, fruit, and vegetables from irrigated land and hunted wild antelope and deer. They raised oxen and buffalo to pull plows and provide milk. They were the first people to grow cotton. Women picked its fluffy fibers, then spun and wove them to make cloth. Along the coast, cotton was also used to make strong fishing nets.

▲ These huge storage jars were found in a royal palace in Crete. They are about 6 feet high and were made to hold oil and grain.

FISHING AND POTTERY

EUROPE

In southern Europe most people were farmers or fishermen. Farmers grew barley, grapes, and olives. Fishermen caught mackerel, tuna, octopus, and squid. There were also many artisans, who lived in towns. Cretan artisans made huge pottery jars, called pithoi, for storing oil, grain, and wine. They also made brightly decorated vases, gold and ivory jewelry, and bronze swords. These were sold in Greece, Egypt, and Middle Eastern lands. In Greece and Crete, towns were built on hilltops and were surrounded by strong stone walls. Town houses were two or three stories high.

▶ This wall painting, or fresco, from Knossos, in Crete, shows a young fisherman with his catch.

◀ Clay models like this ox cart were made as toys and as religious offerings. They tell us what farm life was like in the Indus Valley.

FARMING LIFE

In northern Europe there were no towns. People lived in villages and on small farms. Farmers had to cut down the dense forests before they could clear fields and plant crops of wheat and barley. Farmers kept cattle, sheep, and goats for meat, milk, hides, and wool. They built their houses from local materials such as stone or timber, with reed or straw-thatched roofs. Farming families also ate wild foods, such as birds' eggs, fish from rivers and the ocean, and mushrooms, raspberries, hazelnuts, and plums. In the forests they hunted deer and boar with spears.

FAMILIES

The Shang kings ruled a vast empire based in China's Huang He (Yellow River) valley. The soil was rich and fertile, although buildings and people were often swept away by earthquakes and floods. Most people lived in large villages, surrounded by deep ditches for defense. Parents, children, grandparents, cousins, uncles, and aunts all lived together. Traditionally, the happiest homes had five generations all living under one roof.

▲ In regions where there was not much stone, Chinese builders made walls out of pounded earth supported by a wooden framework. This picture was painted around A.D. 100, but it shows how houses were built even before Tutankhamen's time.

RICH AND POOR

The nobles of China lived a luxurious life. They wore silk clothes, and their houses were full of rich goods, such as bronze jugs and mirrors, and even jade scoops to clean their ears. Bronze was a new invention and was too special to use for farm tools, so peasants still worked using tools made of stone and wood. Peasants wore simple tunics and trousers made of hemp. In the north, where it was cold, they wore thick, padded jackets. Chinese farmers had to pay a tax to their landlord or give him a share of their crops. They also had to work for the government for one month every year.

► Rich farmers built watchtowers to guard their land. This clay model was made in about 200 B.C., but watchtowers like this were being built hundreds of years earlier.

◄ On the steep slopes of the Andes, farmers cut terraces like the ones in this picture to plant their crops of potatoes and corn.

▼ An Aboriginal eel trap, made of woven rushes and willow twigs. Traps like these were hidden among the reeds at the edge of shallow rivers and lakes. This picture was sketched by a nineteenth-century traveler, but archaeologists believe this way of catching eels was invented in Tutankhamen's time.

THE NORTH

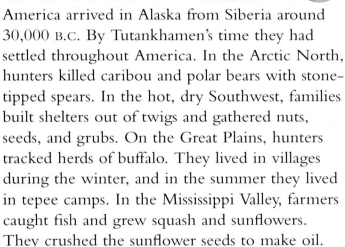
AMERICAS

The first inhabitants of America arrived in Alaska from Siberia around 30,000 B.C. By Tutankhamen's time they had settled throughout America. In the Arctic North, hunters killed caribou and polar bears with stone-tipped spears. In the hot, dry Southwest, families built shelters out of twigs and gathered nuts, seeds, and grubs. On the Great Plains, hunters tracked herds of buffalo. They lived in villages during the winter, and in the summer they lived in tepee camps. In the Mississippi Valley, farmers caught fish and grew squash and sunflowers. They crushed the sunflower seeds to make oil.

EDIBLE DOGS AND GUINEA PIGS

On the dry hillsides of Mexico, the main crop was corn. In the hot, wet valleys farmers grew avocados, beans, tomatoes, and chillies, and raised turkeys and dogs to eat. Ordinary people's homes were made of earth with roofs thatched with leaves. Rulers lived in fine palaces made of stone.

In the Andes, farmers lived in houses made of rough-hewn stone. They dug irrigation channels and planted crops of potatoes and corn. They also raised guinea pigs for food, llamas to carry heavy loads, and alpacas for their warm wool.

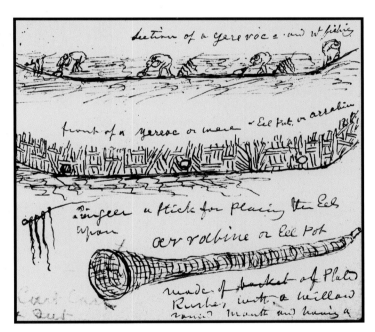

MOTHS AND EELS

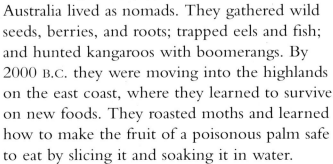
AUSTRALASIA

The Aborigines of Australia lived as nomads. They gathered wild seeds, berries, and roots; trapped eels and fish; and hunted kangaroos with boomerangs. By 2000 B.C. they were moving into the highlands on the east coast, where they learned to survive on new foods. They roasted moths and learned how to make the fruit of a poisonous palm safe to eat by slicing it and soaking it in water.

DISCOVERY AND INVENTION

The years from about 2000 to 1200 B.C. are often called the Bronze Age, because widespread use of bronze from about 2000 B.C. changed people's lives. Bronze is a metal—a mixture of about 90 percent copper and 10 percent tin. Metalworkers in Asia, western Europe, and the Middle East all discovered how to make it at about the same time.

Before bronze was invented, people used knives and weapons made of wood, copper, or stone. But copper was very soft, and stone was heavy and difficult to shape. Bronze was much harder and sharper than copper and could be hammered and molded into intricate shapes. Metalworkers used bronze to make better, stronger swords, shields, daggers, helmets, and spears.

▼ This wall painting from an Egyptian tomb shows a boat on the Nile River. The boat moves with the help of the rowers and by wind trapped in the big square sail.

WATER ENGINEERS

AFRICA

Egyptian civilization was already 2,000 years old in Tutankhamen's time. For hundreds of years Egyptian farmers had dug canals and ditches to control the flow of water from the Nile River, and built huge tanks to store flood water for use in dry seasons. In about 1800 B.C. they began to use a machine called a shaduf, which raised water from ditches and rivers to water their fields.

BUILDING TECHNOLOGY

The Egyptians were expert builders. The great pyramids, where earlier pharaohs were buried, are still wonders of the world. But the biggest building projects of Tutankhamen's time were new cities, temples, palaces, and underground tombs. Builders had only simple tools such as chisels and mallets, but they used them with great skill. They drew accurate plans on papyrus and measured building sites with knotted ropes. They raised huge blocks of stone to the top of buildings by hauling them up ramps of pounded earth.

◄ A scroll of papyrus showing calculations made by an Egyptian mathematician around 1600 B.C. On the left are rules for measuring pyramids, angles, and triangles. On the right are instructions for surveying land.

SUNDIALS AND MEDICINE

To measure time and record events, the Egyptians invented water clocks, sundials, and picture writing called hieroglyphics. These were not new in Tutankhamen's day, but they were always being improved. Mummy-making had also become a more complicated process. As well as preserving bodies, the Egyptians also studied them scientifically and recorded their findings in papyrus scrolls. These were written for doctors and gave details of diseases, treatments, and medicines. Doctors learned a great deal about how the body is made, and also believed that the heart is the center of the body.

◄ An obelisk (tall stone pillar) from the temple built at Karnak, Egypt, by Pharaoh Thutmose III, who ruled from 1504-1450 B.C. It displays the pharaoh's name and his deeds in hieroglyphs.

◀ Babylonian copper farming equipment, including sickles, knives, and axes, made around 1550 B.C. Old-style tools like these were used before bronze and iron tools were invented.

▼ The Babylonians used their mathematical skills for measuring and surveying land. This clay tablet, written in cuneiform (wedge-shaped writing) was made around 1980 B.C. It records the size of five fields.

ASTRONOMERS AND IRON

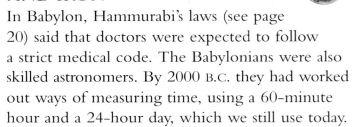

MIDDLE EAST

In Babylon, Hammurabi's laws (see page 20) said that doctors were expected to follow a strict medical code. The Babylonians were also skilled astronomers. By 2000 B.C. they had worked out ways of measuring time, using a 60-minute hour and a 24-hour day, which we still use today.

Some of the most important Middle Eastern inventions were designed for war. Around 1800 B.C. soldiers invented a wheeled battle-chariot, pulled by fast horses. By Tutankhamen's time it had been copied by the Egyptians and other neighboring countries.

In about 1900 B.C. metalworkers in Syria and Turkey discovered how to make weapons and farm tools out of iron. This gave them a great advantage in building and farming, as well as in war. Iron was stronger, sharper, longer-lasting, and more plentiful than bronze or copper. But for a while iron was so rare and valuable—more precious than gold—that only a few people worked with it. Iron only became widely used throughout the Middle East by about 1100 B.C.

A NEW ALPHABET

Around 1100 B.C., the Phoenicians made two important discoveries. They discovered how to produce purple dye using sea snails and a chemical called alum, dug from rocks. The dye was very valuable, and selling it made them rich.

But their second development was even more important. They created an alphabet of letters. It soon replaced earlier ways of writing based on pictures (in Egypt) or patterns of little wedge shapes (in Mesopotamia). The Phoenician alphabet consisted of 22 letters. They were all consonants. Vowels were added later by Greek scholars. We still use the Phoenician alphabet today, in a modern form.

DAMS AND DRAINS

SOUTH ASIA

The people living in the Indus Valley, like the Egyptians and the Mesopotamians, depended on a river for their survival and became skilled water engineers. They were among the first people to build dams to control the flow of water and surrounded their fields with irrigation ditches. They also used careful measurements and engineering to plan and build their big cities. These had complicated underground networks of freshwater pipes and drains. They invented a system of writing, using picture symbols scratched on tablets of damp clay. But a great mystery still surrounds this picture writing. No one has yet been able to work out what it means.

SILK AND BRONZE

EAST ASIA

In Tutankhamen's time, China was isolated from many other parts of the world. The Chinese did not know about inventions in Egypt and the Middle East. But they made their own discoveries to meet their own needs.

According to Chinese legends, the king of Hsia (see page 22) taught people how to control floods, dig irrigation ditches, grow crops, and make medicines. His wife showed people how to spin silk from the cocoons of silkworms. Chinese people knew about all these things by around 2000 B.C. Soon afterward they invented wheeled chariots for war. They also invented the potter's wheel (also invented in Mesopotamia).

By around 1500 B.C., Chinese metalworkers had discovered how to make beautiful vessels out of bronze. Scribes invented a system of picture writing, which is still used as the basis of Chinese script.

By 1000 B.C. they had compiled a dictionary with 40,000 different characters. Chinese scholars also made mathematical discoveries, including an early form of "times tables."

► Chinese designs were copied by artisans in southern Asia. In Thailand they created beautiful pottery like this vase using very simple methods. They did not have potters' wheels, so every pot was carefully smoothed into shape and decorated by hand.

► This Chinese ax head may have been carried by royal bodyguards and fastened to a wooden handle with leather straps. It was made by pouring melted bronze into a clay mold.

MASSIVE MONUMENTS

In northern Europe huge monuments, such as Stonehenge, were enlarged or rebuilt in Tutankhamen's time. Workers had no cranes or pulleys to lift the massive blocks of stone. Instead they used levers to insert a timber platform, or raft, underneath each stone, and then gradually built up the platform from underneath. These monuments were almost certainly designed for religious ceremonies honoring the sun or the moon, but we do not know precisely how they were used.

LAKE VILLAGES

In some parts of Europe, especially Switzerland and northern Italy, people built artificial islands in the middle of deep lakes. They were the safest sites for new village homes. Villagers traveled to and from their fields by boat or walked across well-defended bridges of stones and pounded earth, which linked the villages with the shore.

▲ Stonehenge, a huge circle-shaped monument in southern England. It was rebuilt and enlarged between about 2100 and 1500 B.C. The outer ring measures almost 98 feet across. There are 30 standing stones, called sarsens, all about 14 feet high.

ARCTIC INVENTIONS

Because most Native Americans left no written records, it is hard to know exactly when they made many of their inventions and discoveries. But archaeologists use scientific techniques, such as radiocarbon dating, to help them find out. Their results suggest that by about 1600 B.C. Native Americans in Arctic North America had invented long-bladed knives made of bone, walrus ivory, and wood to cut large blocks of snow for building some of the first igloos. Archaeologists have also found the remains of well-designed kayaks. These sea-going canoes, used to hunt seals and walrus, were first used about 1500 B.C.

JADE AND PYRAMIDS

In about 1200 B.C. the Olmec people of Mexico became very skilled at carving jade—an extremely hard stone. First the jade block was roughly cut using a mallet made from stone. Then the shape was hollowed out and finely polished with grains of wet sand. Workers used the sand to rub away at the surface, because they did not have metal tools. This was very slow and took a lot of hard work. Enormous amounts of labor were also needed to build the Olmecs' pyramid-shaped temples. Archaeologists have worked out that it took 800,000 working days to build the largest pyramid, which dates from around 900 B.C.

Olmec scholars were very skillful astronomers. They worked out a calendar based on the movements of the sun and the moon and invented a system of picture writing to record what they had seen.

PET DINGOES

AUSTRALASIA

Wolf-like dogs called dingoes were first brought to Australia around 2000 B.C., probably by traders from southern Asia. Dingoes could be trained as guard dogs but were mostly treated as pets, especially by women whose babies had died. They were also used to provide warmth in bed, like modern hot-water bottles. A traditional Aborigine saying describes a chilly winter night as "five-dog weather."

◀ This mask of jade was made by Olmec artisans, probably for a priest or a king to wear. Fine, very delicate objects like this took many months to make.

▲ This picture of an Aborigine campsite was painted in the nineteenth century. You can see two dingoes sitting by the campfire.

DEATH SPEARS

Around the same time, Aborigine warriors invented new weapons and used them in battles to conquer new land. Death spears were sticks covered with tiny, razor-sharp blades. They were designed to make their victim bleed to death. A spear-throwing device, called a woomera, was used to throw spears over a long distance.

THE CREATIVE WORLD

▲ This gold ornament is shaped like an eagle with outstretched wings. It was found in the tomb of a Phoenician king. He would have worn it across his chest.

Sometimes people looking back into the past think that societies long ago were primitive and unskilled. This is not true. The people of Tutankhamen's time had not invented many of the machines that make life easy in the modern world. They had no motors and no electricity, no televisions or computers or cars. But they survived without all the technology that helps us today. They not only survived, but using the simplest of tools, they created huge buildings that have lasted thousands of years and beautiful works of art that people still admire.

◀ A tomb painting from Egypt. It shows a dead man and his wife in the next world. They are listening to a musician who is playing the harp and singing. Rich Egyptian people enjoyed watching all kinds of entertainers at parties and feasts, including singers, dancers, jugglers, and acrobats.

PALACES AND TOMBS

AFRICA

The treasures found in Tutankhamen's tomb show the skills of Egyptian artists. These people made beautiful jewels, weapons, furniture, vases, statues, and wall paintings to enrich the pharaohs' palaces, temples, and tombs. They used gold, bronze, turquoise, and cedar wood, brought to their workshops from hundreds of miles away. Hard building stone was often found nearby, but it took thousands of hours of patient work with simple copper, wood, and stone tools to produce temple figures of pharaohs and gods, or delicate carvings to decorate palace walls.

ROYAL TREASURES

MIDDLE EAST

The arts and crafts of many Middle Eastern lands show the luxurious lifestyles of rich and powerful kings. Many everyday items used by royal families in their palaces have survived, as well as crowns, weapons, and jewelry, such as the eagle ornament on page 36. Even drinking cups and musical instruments were often beautifully decorated or trimmed with gold.

Middle Eastern kings also commissioned splendid buildings including ziggurats (pyramid-shaped temples) and palaces with gardens and lakes. Scribes found time to write down religious texts and ancient legends—like the story of Gilgamesh, a mighty hero, who had all kinds of adventures in the kingdom of the gods.

BRONZE AND JADE

EAST ASIA

In China, craft workers made bronze vessels in all kinds of shapes to hold religious offerings. Some looked like animals, others like monsters. Chinese craft workers also carved objects out of the precious green stone called jade, and they made pottery jugs and dishes in fantastic shapes, with delicate decorations. At first these were made for everyday use by kings and nobles, but the best examples were later collected as works of art, just to be admired.

▲ There is a lot of fine detail in this work. It is made from red-colored gold and shows an Egyptian pharaoh riding in his chariot.

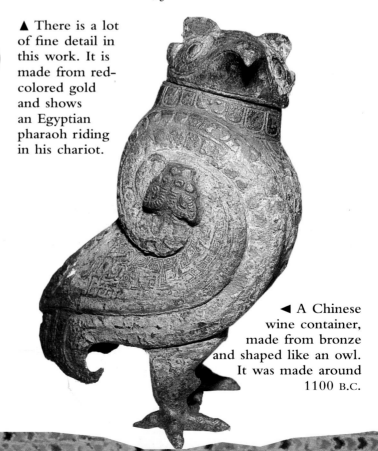

◄ A Chinese wine container, made from bronze and shaped like an owl. It was made around 1100 B.C.

► A stone seal with an elephant carving, made at Mohenjo-Daro in the Indus Valley. The most beautiful seals were worn on necklaces or around the wrist.

FINE DECORATION

In northern Europe, stone monuments such as Stonehenge (see page 34) were built or rebuilt in Tutankhamen's time. They still impress us today with their size and with the boldness and strength of their design. But European craft workers were also capable of detailed, delicate work. They made necklaces out of smooth, shiny amber, which they collected from the seashore, and collars and bracelets of glittering gold. They cast finely decorated swords, axes, helmets, and shields by pouring molten bronze into carved stone molds.

◄ Artists took many of their ideas from the world around them. This pottery jar from Mycenae, Greece, is painted with an octopus design.

ALL KINDS OF CRAFTS

Visitors to the workshops at Mohenjo-Daro, the biggest city in the Indus Valley region, would have met many different artisans: metalworkers, potters, bead makers, and cloth makers. Stone carvers engraved scenes of religious worship or everyday life onto tiny seal stones, about 1 inch long. When these seal stones were pressed into melted wax, they left a little picture. Seals were used to approve documents or to seal bags holding valuable goods. Craft workers also made toys, whistles, and lifelike statues out of clay. All these goods were traded with other Indus Valley cities and with neighboring lands. Examples of standardized weights and measures, to keep traders from cheating, have also been found in Indus Valley sites.

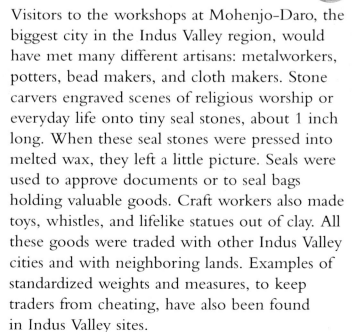

PAINTINGS AND POTTERY

In southern Europe many wall paintings, statues, and painted pots have survived to tell us about the people who lived in the rich Minoan and Mycenean civilizations of Greece, and what kinds of decorations they admired. Artists painted frescoes using paint and water on damp plaster walls to create very fresh colors. There is an example on page 15. On mainland Greece, kings and chieftains lived in well-defended palaces, decorated with carved lions and other ferocious creatures, which were designed to display a ruler's strength and power. Kings were buried with a large quantity of rich grave goods so they could go on enjoying their treasures in the kingdom of the dead.

EARTHWORKS AND WEAVING

In parts of the Americas massive earthworks and huge stone monuments were an important form of art. They still survive today at Chavín de Huántar in Peru and in southeastern North America. Some of the earliest South American pottery and cloth was made in Peru between 2000 and 1000 B.C. Weavers in Peru were usually women. They made beautiful fabrics, often patterned with designs of jaguars, and woven in strong colors that can still be seen today.

MAGIC SCENES

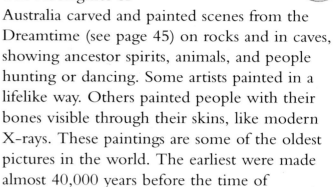

The Aborigines of Australia carved and painted scenes from the Dreamtime (see page 45) on rocks and in caves, showing ancestor spirits, animals, and people hunting or dancing. Some artists painted in a lifelike way. Others painted people with their bones visible through their skins, like modern X-rays. These paintings are some of the oldest pictures in the world. The earliest were made almost 40,000 years before the time of Tutankhamen, although they were still being created during his reign.

Artists used two methods to create pictures. They either rubbed colored earth onto the cave's rocky walls, or they crushed the earth to a fine powder and blew it through pipes to make patterns on the surface of the cave wall.

▲ An Aborigine painting from Nourlangie Rock, Australia. It shows figures from the Dreamtime, painted in X-ray style.

► This painted pot shows women weaving cloth on a backstrap loom—a simple, lightweight, portable invention that is still used today.

BELIEFS AND IDEAS

P eople living in the time of Tutankhamen thought the world was a frightening and unpredictable place. When floods, earthquakes, and storms wrecked fields and farms and disease killed thousands of people, no one understood why. They felt helpless and feared they had upset the gods or the invisible spirits who controlled their land. To keep these disasters from happening again, they held ceremonies to please the gods and spirits and offered them gifts of their most precious things: their children, their best animals, wine, and food. People living in different parts of the world worshiped their own special gods and goddesses in different ways. But they usually shared many of the same beliefs and fears. Often they tried to get close to their gods by singing, dancing, meditating, or taking drugs. To prepare for these religious ceremonies, they purified themselves by taking special baths or fasting.

▲ This necklace from Tutankhamen's tomb is decorated with gold and stone scarab beetles. These beetles collect little balls of dung and roll them across the ground. The Egyptians thought they were holy creatures because their movements were like the movements of the sun god as he rolled the sun across the sky.

◄ An Egyptian painting on papyrus shows the jackal-headed god, Anubis, making a mummy. The storage jars beneath the mummy hold the dead person's heart, liver, and other organs.

LIFE AND DEATH

The Egyptians believed in life after death. That is why they preserved people's bodies as mummies. They thought that a person's spirit would live in the next world only for as long as his or her mummified body survived. First the body was washed and the organs removed. Then it was dried out, using a chemical called natron, and refilled with sawdust, linen, resin, and natron. Finally, the body was wrapped in linen. Mummies of pharaohs had to be done very well so they would live forever. At first ordinary people were not mummified but were buried.

POWERFUL GODS

AFRICA

Egyptian people believed that the gods had created the world and continued to rule it, so everyone had to live by their laws. This meant fighting bravely, working hard, and making offerings to the gods. The ancient Egyptians worshiped many different gods and goddesses. Each one looked after a particular part of daily life or was linked to powerful natural forces, such as the sun or storms.

SACRED SPIRITS

Many African people were animists. Animists believed that all living and natural things, including rocks and mountains, had powerful spirits. They made offerings to please these spirits or to ask for their help. They also honored their dead ancestors, who had the power to bring disaster if angered or ignored. Priests performed ceremonies to help them see into the future and to drive away evil spirits.

► Egyptian craft workers made wooden boxes to hold shabti figures. These were buried with mummies to look after them in the kingdom of the dead. The box is decorated with a picture of a priestess kneeling in front of Nut, the sky goddess.

STAIRWAYS TO HEAVEN

MIDDLE EAST

The peoples of Mesopotamia worshiped gods and goddesses they believed had many different powers. Marduk made crops grow, Sin was god of the moon, and Ishtar was goddess of war. The gods protected individual men and women and whole cities, too. But they also had terrible powers to punish or destroy. Mesopotamian people offered sacrifices and said prayers at the top of huge ziggurats. These were pyramid-shaped temples, built as high as possible to reach up to the gods. People called them "stairways to heaven."

► A carved stone stele (pillar), made around 1900 B.C. in Canaan. It shows the god Baal, lord of storms. He is armed with a thunderbolt, ready to attack his enemies.

▲ The Great Ziggurat at Ur, in present-day Iraq, was built around 2100 B.C. It was still used for ceremonies hundreds of years later, in Tutankhamen's day.

HIGH ALTARS

In Canaan and nearby lands, the Philistines worshiped El, god of the sky; Baal, god of winds and thunder; and Baal's wife, Ashtoreth, goddess of love. To feel nearer to the gods, the Philistines built altars on top of high hills. The Jews, who lived in present-day Israel, were unlike many other Middle Eastern peoples. They worshiped only one god. They called him Yaweh.

ORACLE BONES

EAST ASIA

In Shang times, Chinese people believed in a supreme god called Shang Di, who lived in the sky. He sent blessings to people on earth, especially to the Shang emperor, whose official name was "son of heaven." The emperors had to act as a link between heaven and earth by saying prayers and offering sacrifices.

Each Chinese family also believed that the spirits of dead ancestors had the power to help or harm them. The Shang emperors often asked their ancestors for advice. They wrote messages on animal bones or tortoise shells, then heated them. They believed the pattern of cracks that appeared would tell them the future.

◄ An oracle bone from the Shang dynasty in China. You can see the cracks made when it was heated, over 3,000 years ago.

SUN WORSHIPERS

In Japan the ancient national religion was called Shinto. It was based on the worship of gods and nature spirits, such as Amaterasu, the sun goddess. Shinto taught that every natural object had a spirit that should be respected. Japanese people also honored their emperors, and believed they were descended from the sun goddess. Family ancestors and national heroes were also honored with offerings. Shinto is still a principle religion of Japan.

MOTHER OF THE WORLD

SOUTH ASIA

The Indus Valley people worshiped a goddess they called Mother of the World. She gave life to all creatures. They also worshiped a male god. We don't know his name, but he later became known as Shiva in the Hindu faith. He was worshiped as both a creator and a destroyer. One of his names is Lord of the Dance.

Fire and water were important in Indus Valley religious ceremonies. People killed animals and burned them as offerings. Priests and priest kings purified themselves in sacred baths before taking part in religious rituals. Farther south, Indian worshipers honored idols by sprinkling them with perfume and decorating them with flowers.

THE ARYANS

In about 1500 B.C., invaders known as the Aryan people brought a new religion to northern India. They worshiped nature gods such as Indra, god of the sky; Agni, god of fire; Surya, the sun god; and Yama, god of death. Aryan priests and poets composed a series of religious songs known as the Rig-Veda, which means "verses of knowledge." They are among the oldest surviving poems in the world and tell stories about gods and heroes. Because ordinary people could not read or write, poems and songs were the best way of teaching everyone about beliefs and ideas.

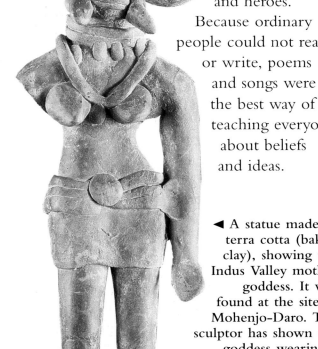

◄ A statue made of terra cotta (baked clay), showing the Indus Valley mother goddess. It was found at the site of Mohenjo-Daro. The sculptor has shown the goddess wearing a magnificent headdress, several necklaces, and a short skirt.

CELTIC GODS

In northern Europe some early Celtic peoples believed in many different gods and goddesses, who protected and helped them. In return, the Celts offered sacrifices to the gods of horses, weapons, jewels, and people. Victims for sacrifice were thrown into lakes or bogs. The Celts also preserved the skulls of ancestors and enemies. They believed that a person's spirit stayed in the head after death and would protect the living.

BULL LEAPING

In Crete, palaces were built with central courtyards where bull-leaping ceremonies were held. Specially trained athletes captured from conquered cities had to vault through the horns of a bull as it charged around. This was terribly dangerous, and many athletes died. At the end of the ceremony, the bull was also killed. The Cretans believed that this bloodshed helped to bring a good harvest the following year.

JAGUAR BABY

The many different peoples of North America had similar religious ideas. They respected the living world and tried to live in harmony with it. They honored Mother Earth and the invisible spirits they believed dwelled in mountains, winds, and trees. Totem animals were important, too. They guided and protected individuals and tribes.

In Mexico the Olmecs carved many images of their special god—part human infant and part jaguar. He was powerful and bloodthirsty, with fearsome fangs. The Olmecs also worshiped other fierce animal gods. These represented the animals that lived in the rain forest around them, including alligators, snakes, and sharks.

▼ This fresco (wall painting) was made for the palace of King Minos in Crete. It shows three athletes taking part in the bull-leaping ritual to bring a good harvest.

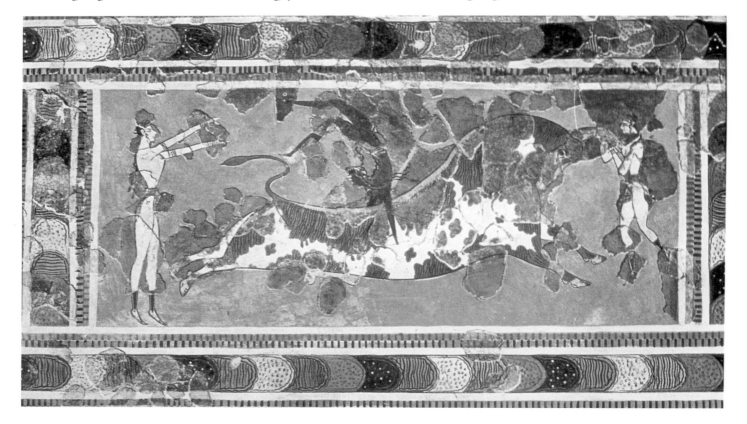

▲ In this Olmec stone carving you can see a king carrying a "were-jaguar" god in his arms. Carvings like this show that the Olmecs believed some of their kings were descended from the gods and had magical powers, including being able to take either human or jaguar shape.

GODS FOR SURVIVAL

In South America, people said prayers to a creator god. They believed he was ruler of the world and lord of the sun. In the Andes region they called him Viracocha, but people gave him different names elsewhere.

South American people also honored many other nature gods as providers of good harvests and life-giving rain. These were essential for survival, so South American priests and people took part in special ceremonies at important times in the farming year, such as at planting or harvest. They also offered sacrifices of people or blood to please the gods.

DREAMTIME

In Australia, religious beliefs came from the idea of the Dreamtime. This was a magical era when the ancestors of all living creatures walked and danced on earth. The ancestors bound together all parts of creation—land, sky, water, people, animals, and plants—to make a peaceful whole. Aborigines held religious ceremonies at holy sites, such as the great rock Uluru, recreating their ancestors' dances to maintain good order in the world.

NATURE GODS

On the islands of the Pacific Ocean, people were afraid of the powerful creatures around them, such as sharks, and of natural forces, such as lightning and volcanoes. People thought of these as nature gods and made images to honor the gods so that the natural world would not harm them.

► A modern carving of a sea spirit with a shark's head. It is made from wood and comes from the Solomon Islands in the Pacific Ocean. There are no ancient carvings like these left, because wood does not last as long as stone, but ancient traditions continue.

GLOSSARY

PEOPLES FROM AROUND THE WORLD

Aborigines The first inhabitants of Australia, who arrived there about 40,000 years ago.

Aryans A subgroup of the Indo-European people. They migrated to India around 1500 B.C.

Bantu People who lived in the rain forests and plains of central and southern Africa.

Celts Hunters and farmers who lived in northern Europe.

Chavín Farmers who lived in the mountains of Peru around 1200 B.C.

Hebrews People who settled in ancient Israel (parts of present-day Israel, Syria, and Jordan) around 1000 B.C.

Hittites People who settled in Anatolia (present-day Turkey) around 2000 B.C.

Hyksos Groups of invaders from Asia who ruled Egypt about 150 years before Tutankhamen was born.

Indo-Europeans A term to describe many prehistoric peoples of Europe, central Asia, and northern India.

Inuit Native Americans who arrived in the Arctic regions of North America from Siberia around 2000 B.C.

Khoisan Nomad hunters and gatherers from southern Africa.

Minoans The people who lived on the Mediterranean island of Crete from around 2000–1450 B.C.

Mongols Nomads from the grassy plains north of China.

Myceneans People who lived in and around the city-state of Mycenae, southern Greece, from about 1600–1100 B.C.

Native Americans The first inhabitants of America, who arrived there about 30,000 years ago. Native American people were divided into many nations, with different lifestyles and languages.

Olmecs The people who lived in the coastal lowlands of southern Mexico from around 2000 B.C.

Pacific peoples People who lived on islands in the Pacific Ocean. They were descended from settlers who migrated there from southeastern Asia.

Phoenicians People who lived along the eastern Mediterranean coast. From around 1100 B.C. they built up a rich trading empire.

Sumerians People who settled in southern Mesopotamia from around 3500 B.C. They built some of the world's earliest cities and invented writing.

alpaca South American animal of the camel family.

amber Sticky, yellowish gum produced by trees. Over many years it becomes hard and is used to make jewelry.

archaeologist A person who studies the ancient past by digging up remains.

astronomer A scientist who studies the stars and planets.

burial mound A mound, usually made of earth, under which people were buried.

calculation Mathematical workings out.

cast To shape liquid metal or glass by pouring it into a mold.

ceremony A formal gathering of people, often with music, held in honor of a special event.

chariot A two-wheeled vehicle pulled by horses.

chieftain Leader of a tribe or group of people often related by birth or marriage.

city-state A city or town, together with the surrounding farms and fields.

civilization A society with its own laws, customs, beliefs, and artistic traditions.

cocoon A case of silky thread spun by larvae of insects in which they develop.

code A series of laws or rules gathered into one set of instructions.

democratic Describes a country in which the people choose the leaders who govern them.

dye A mixture used to color things. In Tutankhamen's time, dyes were made of plants, crushed rocks, and metal shavings.

earthwork A large mound, ditch, bank, or circle that is made of earth dug from the land around.

embroidered Decorated with patterns and pictures sewn in colored threads.

empire A large area of land, including several different nations or peoples, governed by a single ruler called an emperor.

engrave Cut into a hard surface.

fortress A building that is strongly defended against attack.

gourds Plants with fruits that can be dried, hollowed out, and used as containers.

grave goods Valuable objects buried with a dead person.

hemp Rough cloth made from plant fibres.

hieroglyphs Ancient Egyptian picture writing.

Hindu A follower of the Hindu religion, which began in India between around 1500 and 600 B.C. Hindus worship many gods, but they are all forms of Brahma, the supreme god.

inlaid Set into a surface.

irrigation The channelling of water into dry land so that crops can grow there.

ivory The hard substance that elephant and walrus tusks are made of.

llama South American animal of the camel family.

meditate Think deeply about spiritual things.

memorial A building or object made in honor of a dead person or past event.

Middle East The term used to describe an area stretching east from the Mediterranean Sea.

migration The movement of many people together in search of new lands.

mummy A body that has been specially preserved before burial.

navigate To plot a course at sea and steer a ship along it.

nomads People who have no settled home, and who move from place to place in search of food or grazing land.

oracle A telling of future events through special signs.

papyrus Paper made from the papyrus reed.

pharaoh The name for a king in Ancient Egypt.

plantain A bananalike fruit with a green skin.

primitive Lacking knowledge or skills.

pulley A wheel with a grooved rim in which a rope can run. A series of pulleys can be used to lift heavy loads.

purify To free oneself from bad behavior or thoughts. People thought they could do this by washing or going without food.

radiocarbon dating A way of discovering how old some remains are by measuring the amount of radioactive carbon in them.

resin Sticky gum produced by trees.

ritual Traditional way of marking a special, often religious, event.

sacrifice An offering made to please the gods.

scholar Someone who spends his or her life studying.

scribe A specially trained person who kept written records of events, business deals, laws and so on.

scroll Word used for a roll of paper, parchment, or papyrus.

seal Stamp or design pressed into clay or wax to show ownership or official approval.

sesame A plant grown for its seeds, which are eaten or crushed to make oil.

shaman A magic healer.

sickle A curved knife used to cut crops.

squash A food plant of the gourd family.

sundial A kind of clock that uses the sun's shadow to tell the time.

survey To measure land by working out distances and area mathematically.

technology The science of developing tools and techniques to meet practical needs.

teepee The Native American name for a tent made of animal skins and wooden poles.

totem An object that represents a family or tribe.

tribe A group of peoples of the same race and culture.

vizier An important official in the Egyptian government.

warlord A warrior leader who controls parts of a country.

yam A kind of root vegetable.

INDEX